Kids' Birthday Cakes

Spectacular cakes for that special day

Love Food ® is an imprint of Parragon Books Ltd

Parragon
Queen Street House
4 Queen Street
Bath BA1 1HE, UK

ISBN 978-1-4075-2500-6

Printed in China

Produced by the Buenavista Studio s.l.
Text and Recipes by Oliver Trific
Edited by Fiona Biggs
Photography by Günter Beer
Home Economy by Stevan Paul
Design by Cammaert & Eberhardt

Notes for the reader

This book uses both metric and imperial measurements. Follow the same units of measurement throughout; do not mix metric and imperial. All spoon measurements are level, unless otherwise stated: teaspoons are assumed to be 5 ml and tablespoons are assumed to be 15 ml. Unless otherwise stated, milk is assumed to be semi-skimmed, eggs and individual vegetables such as potatoes are medium, and pepper is freshly ground black pepper.
The times given are an approximate guide only. Preparation times differ according to the techniques used by different people and the cooking times may also vary from those given. Optional ingredients, variations or serving suggestions have not been included in the calculations.
Recipes using raw or very lightly cooked eggs should be avoided by infants, the elderly, pregnant women, convalescents and anyone suffering from an illness. Pregnant and breasfeeding women advised to avoid eating peanuts and peanut products.Sufferers from nut allergies should be aware that some of ready-made ingredients used in the recipes in this book may contain nuts. Always check the packaging before use.

Contents

The Basics   6

The Cakes   24

Index   64

The Basics

Birthday cakes naturally need to taste as good as they look. Moist cake and creamy icing are the delicious canvas for the whimsical creations in this book. The following recipes are simple, quick and taste just great.

Chocolate Cake

115 g/4 oz unsalted butter, melted, plus extra for greasing

240 g/8½ oz plain flour, plus extra for dusting

350 g/12 oz granulated sugar

2 large eggs

85 g/3 oz cocoa powder

1½ tsp baking powder

1½ tsp bicarbonate of soda

1 tsp salt

250 ml/9 fl oz milk (or half milk and half soured cream)

2 tsp vanilla extract

250 ml/9 fl oz boiling water

Everyone loves a chocolate cake. The scent of chocolate is difficult to resist, even more so if the cake is covered with rich, creamy icing.

Makes 1 large cake or 2 small cakes

Bring the refrigerated ingredients to room temperature. Preheat the oven to 180°C/350°F/Gas Mark 4. Grease a 25 x 30-cm/10 x 12-inch rectangular cake tin or two 20–23-cm/8–9-inch round cake tins, line with baking paper and grease and flour the paper. Dust the inside of the tin with flour and tap out the excess.

Using an electric mixer, cream the butter and sugar until smooth and light in colour. Beat in one egg at a time, ensuring that each is completely incorporated into the mixture before adding the next.

Sift the cocoa powder, flour, baking powder, bicarbonate of soda and salt into a separate bowl. Add the cocoa mixture to the mixing bowl alternately with the milk, then add the vanilla extract and beat on medium speed for 2 minutes. Add the boiling water and beat to combine well (the mixture will be on the thin side). Pour into the prepared tin.

Place the tin in the centre of the oven and bake for 30–35 minutes or until a skewer inserted in the centre of the cake comes out clean. Remove from the oven and leave to cool in the tin on a cooling rack. After 10 minutes, loosen the cake from the sides of the tin with a palette knife, shake the tin to make sure the cake is not sticking to it and invert onto a cooling rack. Remove the baking paper and leave to cool completely before icing.

Banana Cake

unsalted butter, for greasing

280 g/10 oz plain flour, plus extra for dusting

¾ tsp bicarbonate of soda

1 tsp baking powder

½ tsp salt

4 bananas

2 large eggs

200 g/7 oz granulated sugar

115 ml/3¾ fl oz vegetable oil

1 tsp vanilla extract

125 ml/4 fl oz buttermilk

Bananas turn a simple white cake into a moist sensation. Rich and delicious, this cake goes perfectly with any 'exotic' icing, such as Cream Cheese Coconut Icing (see page 20).

Makes 1 large cake or 2 small cakes

Preheat the oven to 180°C/350°F/Gas Mark 4. Grease a 25 x 30-cm/10 x 12-inch rectangular cake tin or two 20–23-cm/8–9-inch round cake tins, line with baking paper and grease and flour the paper. Dust the inside of the tin with flour and tap out the excess.

Sift the flour, bicarbonate of soda, baking powder and salt into a bowl and set aside. Peel the bananas and mash with a fork.

Using an electric mixer set at medium speed, beat the eggs and sugar together until fluffy and light. Add the oil, then the vanilla extract and mix well. Add the mashed bananas and continue beating until well blended.

Pour in the flour mixture and buttermilk alternately, starting and finishing with the flour mixture. Mix until just blended, then pour into the prepared tin.

Place the tin on the centre rack of the oven and bake for 30 minutes or until a skewer comes out clean. Remove from the oven and leave to cool on a cooling rack. When cool, loosen the cake from the sides of the tin, invert, remove the baking paper and reinvert back onto the rack. Leave to cool completely before cutting into layers and icing.

Soured Cream Madeira Cake

225 g/8 oz unsalted butter, cut into small pieces, plus extra for greasing

425 g/15 oz plain flour, plus extra for dusting

½ tsp baking powder

¼ tsp bicarbonate of soda

½ tsp salt

600 g/1 lb 5 oz granulated sugar

6 large eggs

1 tsp vanilla extract

1 tsp lemon extract (or grated rind of 1 lemon, if preferred)

225 ml/8 fl oz soured cream

Tangy soured cream adds a rich new flavour dimension to traditional Madeira cake.

Makes 1 cake

Preheat the oven to 160°C/325°F/Gas Mark 3. Bring the refrigerated ingredients to room temperature. Grease a 25-cm/10-inch fluted tube tin or Bundt ring, line with baking paper and grease and flour the paper. Dust the inside of the ring with flour and tap out the excess.

Sift the flour, baking powder, bicarbonate of soda and salt into a bowl. In a second bowl, using an electric mixer set at medium speed, beat the butter and sugar together for 3–4 minutes until fluffy and light. Beat in one egg at a time, ensuring that each is completely incorporated into the mixture before adding the next. Add the vanilla extract and lemon extract.

Add a third of the flour mixture to the butter mixture, add half of the soured cream and beat. Continue to add the flour and the remaining soured cream, finishing with the final portion of flour. Scrape the sides of the mixing bowl once or twice with a rubber or silicone spatula to incorporate all the mixture.

Pour the mixture into the tin and smooth it out evenly. Tap the underside of the tin repeatedly to release any air trapped in the mixture. Place the tin in the oven and bake for 1 hour 15 minutes, or until a skewer comes out clean when inserted in the cake.

Remove the cake from the oven and leave to cool for at least 15 minutes on a cooling rack. Gently invert the cake onto a second rack, remove the baking paper and leave to cool completely before icing.

Cook's Tip: if you have more mixture than your tin can hold, leave space at the top, pour the remaining mixture into a second small cake tin and bake separately.

Carrot Cake

unsalted butter or olive oil/water spray, for greasing

280 g/10 oz plain flour, plus extra for dusting

125 g/4½ oz walnut pieces

400 g/14 oz granulated sugar

2 tsp bicarbonate of soda

1 tsp baking powder

1 tbsp ground cinnamon

½ tsp salt

3 large eggs, at room temperature

225 ml/8 fl oz vegetable oil

500 g/1 lb 2 oz carrots, grated

225 g/8 oz crushed pineapple, well drained

Grated carrot and chopped walnuts make this cake a tasty treat. Simply irresistible, it will turn even the most staunch carrot cake doubter into a believer. And, best of all, because it is made in a food processor, it is almost as quick to prepare as it is to eat!

Makes 1 cake

Preheat the oven to 180°C/350°F/Gas Mark 4. Grease a 25-cm/10-inch springform cake tin, line with baking paper and grease and flour the paper. Dust the inside of the tin with flour and tap out the excess.

Process the walnuts in a food processor for several seconds until chopped into small pieces, and set aside.

Using the blade attachment, combine all the dry ingredients in the food processor for 10 seconds. Add the eggs and the oil, and process for an additional 30 seconds. Remove and pour into a large mixing bowl.

Add the walnut pieces, grated carrot and crushed pineapple to the mixture and stir until well blended – the mixture will be very thick.

Pour the mixture into the prepared tin and place on the centre rack of the oven. Bake for 60–70 minutes or until a skewer inserted in the centre of the cake comes out clean.

Allow the cake to cool in the tin on a cooling rack for at least 15 minutes. With a palette knife, gently separate the sides of the cake from the tin. Release the spring latch and remove the side of the tin. Place the rack over the cake top, flip over and remove the tin base and the baking paper. Allow to cool thoroughly before cutting.

Yogurt Sponge Cake

175 g/6 oz unsalted butter, at room temperature, cut into small pieces, plus extra for greasing

350 g/12 oz plain flour, plus extra for dusting

275 g/9½ oz granulated sugar

3 large eggs

1 tsp baking powder

1 tsp bicarbonate of soda

¾ tsp salt

225 ml/8 fl oz natural yogurt

2 tsp vanilla extract

½ tsp almond extract

Moist, with just the right amount of sweetness, this cake is the perfect foundation for any type of icing. But it is delicious on its own, as well!

Makes 1 large cake or 2 small cakes

Bring all the refrigerated ingredients to room temperature. Preheat the oven to 180°C/350°F/Gas Mark 4. Grease a 10 x 12-inch/25 x 30-cm rectangular cake tin or two 20–23-cm/8–9-inch round cake tins, line with baking paper and grease and flour the paper. Dust the inside of the tin with flour and tap out the excess.

Using an electric mixer, cream the butter and sugar until smooth and light in colour. Beat in one egg at a time, ensuring that each is completely incorporated into the mixture before adding the next. Scrape the sides of the mixing bowl with a rubber or silicone spatula once or twice to incorporate all the mixture.

Sift the dry ingredients into a bowl and set aside. In another bowl, combine the yogurt, vanilla extract and almond extract and whisk together.

Add the dry ingredients and the yogurt mixture alternately to the cake mixture in the mixing bowl, ladling in large spoonfuls of each, starting and finishing with the flour. Mix until just well blended. Pour into the prepared tin and place in the centre of the preheated oven. Bake for 35 minutes or until a skewer inserted in the centre of the cake comes out clean.

Remove from the oven and leave to cool on a cooling rack. Gently loosen the cake from the sides of the tin and tap the tin a few times to make sure the cake separates from it. Invert onto the cooling rack, remove the baking paper and leave to cool completely. Ice the cake when it is completely cooled.

Buttercream Icing

Buttercream can be made in advance and stored, tightly covered, in a cool place for up to 1 day. It may not be suitable when outdoor temperatures are very high, but a buttercream-iced cake can be stored in the refrigerator until needed.

Makes enough to ice 1 cake

225 g/8 oz unsalted butter, softened

500 g/1 lb 2 oz icing sugar, sifted

2–3 tbsp milk

1 tsp vanilla extract

For white icing

Using an electric mixer with the paddle attachment or a hand-held electric mixer with the egg beater attachment, beat the butter until light and fluffy. Sift the icing sugar twice and add to the butter with the milk and vanilla extract. Fold in carefully, then beat until pale and creamy. Add more milk if necessary. The consistency should be marshmallow-like, easy to handle but not liquid. Colour the buttercream with food colouring, if desired.

For chocolate icing

Melt 115 g/4 oz of good-quality chocolate in an ovenproof bowl set over a saucepan of simmering water. Remove from the heat and leave to cool but not harden. Beat the cooled chocolate into the Buttercream Icing, or dissolve 1 tablespoon of cocoa powder in 1–2 tablespoons of hot water. Leave to cool and beat into the Buttercream Icing. If adding melted chocolate or cocoa powder, reduce the milk by half when making the basic icing.

Dark Chocolate Icing

Deep, dark chocolate flavour rolled into a buttery icing, this is a dream icing for chocolate lovers.

Makes enough to ice 1 cake

225 g/8 oz unsalted butter, softened

55–85 g/2–3 oz cocoa powder

325 g/11½ oz icing sugar

5 tbsp milk, plus extra if needed

1 tsp vanilla extract

Using an electric mixer with the paddle attachment or a hand-held electric mixer with the egg beater attachment, beat the butter until light and fluffy.

Sift together the cocoa powder and icing sugar and add to the butter, together with the milk and vanilla extract. Fold in carefully, then beat until creamy and spreadable. Add more milk in small amounts until the desired consistency is reached.

Refrigerate, covered, until ready to use.

Cream Cheese Coconut Icing

Cream cheese icing is a perennial favourite, and the shredded coconut gives this version a completely new twist. Try it on the Carrot Cake or the Banana Cake.

Makes enough to ice 1 cake

450 g/1 lb cream cheese, at room temperature

115 g/4 oz unsalted butter, at room temperature

1½ tsp vanilla extract

250 g/9 oz icing sugar, sifted

2 tbsp milk

40 g/1½ oz shredded coconut

Using an electric mixer, beat the cream cheese, butter and vanilla extract in a large bowl until smooth. Add the icing sugar a third at a time, beating well. Stir in the milk and coconut, and mix. The icing can be used immediately or refrigerated until ready to use.

Whipped Soured Cream Icing

This is the perfect icing when you are short of time. Prepare this icing directly when needed and serve the cake as soon as possible, since the whipped cream does not hold up for long.

Makes enough to ice 1 cake

225 ml/8 fl oz double cream

120 g/4¼ oz icing sugar

225 ml/8 fl oz soured cream or natural yogurt

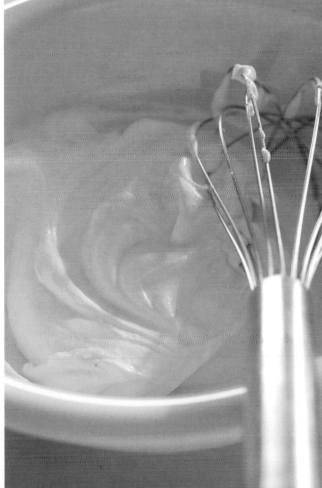

Beat the cream while slowly adding the icing sugar. Continue to beat until soft peaks form. Remove from the mixer and fold in the soured cream. Refrigerate until ready to use.

Cook's Tip: when using the icing as a filling between two cake layers, spread it on the bottom layer to within 2.5 cm/1 inch of the edges because the icing is soft and will ooze out of the sides when the layers are pressed together.

Decorating Marzipan

Possibly of Persian origin, marzipan is a mixture of ground almonds and sugar, mixed together to create a deliciously sweet confection.

Makes enough to cover 1 cake

175 g/6 oz ready-to-roll marzipan

85 g/3 oz icing sugar, plus extra for dusting

food colouring, as desired

Mix the marzipan with the icing sugar and gently knead until smooth. Divide into smaller amounts and colour, as desired, with food colouring. Knead thoroughly for solid colour marzipan – combining less well will result in a streaky effect.

Dust the work surface with icing sugar to prevent the marzipan sticking to the surface. Be generous because the marzipan will absorb a little of the sugar when worked. When the desired colour has been achieved, stop working the marzipan because it will become slightly crumbly if kneaded excessively.

When incorporating the icing sugar into the marzipan, take care not to knead too forcefully because this will cause the marzipan to separate and become crumbly. Subsequently, too much kneading should also be avoided.

As a basic guideline, use 2 parts marzipan to 1 part icing sugar (for example 280 g/10 oz marzipan to 140 g/5 oz icing sugar). Adding more icing sugar will create a stiffer modelling marzipan, which can be helpful if you are creating figures with limbs, rose stems, etc.

You can keep marzipan, covered, in a cool place for up to 1 day.

Cook's Tip: it is best to wear latex gloves when working with marzipan and food colouring, to avoid getting dye on your fingers.

The Cakes

The following chapter contains loads of inspiring cake designs for kids of all ages. Go on – make their day extra special with a cake that looks every bit as fantastic as it tastes.

Alphabet Block Cake

1 quantity Yogurt Sponge Cake
(see page 16)

2 quantities Buttercream Icing
– white (see page 18)

food colouring in desired colours,
to colour icing

Make baby's first birthday special with this delightful, easy-to-make cake. If you are short of time, you can use tubes of prepared coloured icing to decorate the cake.

Bake the cake in a 23-cm/9-inch square cake tin. Leave to cool completely before icing.

Colour the icing with different shades of food colouring. When adding colours to the icing, start with only a few drops of food colouring and mix it into a small amount of icing. Add more icing or colouring until you reach the desired colour.

Cut the cake in half horizontally. Ice the top of one of the layers, place the other layer on top and ice the top and sides of the cake with one quantity of icing.

Using a ruler or straight edge, divide the cake into 9 sections and make a small indentation with the ruler, as if you were creating a noughts-and-crosses grid. This determines the outline of the blocks.

Colour the remaining icing as desired (with at least 3 colours) and transfer the icing to separate piping bags equipped with small-holed nozzles. Outline a box within each section, about 5 mm/¼ inch in from the ruler indentations, alternating the colours as you decorate.

Pipe the numbers, letters or designs into every box. Decorate the sides of the cake in the same way.

Cook's Tip: decorate the cake free-hand for a more child-like appearance.

Flying Balloons Cake

1 quantity Yogurt Sponge Cake
(see page 16)

1 quantity Buttercream Icing
– white (see page 18)

1 quantity Decorating Marzipan
(see page 22)

food colouring, as needed

60-cm/24-inch black liquorice
string

Brighten up any birthday party with this colourful cake. The balloons are simple to make and will definitely catch the eye of the birthday boy or girl.

Bake the cake in a 30-cm/12-inch round cake tin. Leave to cool completely before icing.

When cooled, cut the cake in half horizontally. Ice the top of one half. Place the second half on top of the first and use the remaining icing to ice the top layer evenly. Use a palette knife to create a very even surface.

Create 3–5 different-coloured marzipan mixtures. Roll each into a cylinder and cut into discs. Leave the discs round, or shape them into ovals. Place the discs on the cake. Cut the liquorice string into 5-cm/2-inch lengths and place them on the cake to create the balloon strings. Vary the lengths if desired.

Cook's Tip: you can make a long marzipan ribbon to wrap around the cake by preparing the basic marzipan recipe (see page 22) for decorating and rolling it thin on a floured work surface. Using a pizza wheel, cut the marzipan into strips. Place them around the cake for the ribbon, connecting the ends as necessary.

Teddy Bear Cake

2 quantities Yogurt Sponge Cake
(see page 16)

unsalted butter, for greasing

plain flour, for dusting

1 quantity Buttercream Icing
– white (see page 18)

brown and yellow food colouring

1 quantity Decorating Marzipan
(see page 22)

two-toned jelly sweets

This friendly bear will delight the youngest guests at any birthday party. You can also use real hats, ribbons or bows to decorate it.

Prepare a 25-cm/10-inch springform cake tin and 3 paper cupcake cases. Grease the cake tin, line with baking paper, and grease and flour the paper. Dust the inside of the tin with flour and tap out the excess. Divide the mixture among the prepared tin and paper cases and bake, reducing the baking time to approximately 15–20 minutes for the cupcakes.

Cool the cakes in the tin and paper cases for 15 minutes. Invert the cakes onto cooling racks, remove the baking paper and leave to cool for 1 hour, or until completely cooled.

In a small bowl, dye the icing with brown and yellow colourings to make the desired golden colour for the bear; blend well.

Ice the large cake and place with the flat end down on a serving platter. Ice the small cakes, placing two at the top of the head to form the bear's ears and one in the middle of the cake to form the snout.

Cut some marzipan into thin strips and reserve. Dye the remaining marzipan brown, and shape the eyes, eyebrows, nose and mouth of the bear. Place on the cake. Place the reserved marzipan strips on the eyes. Use jelly sweets to form a bow on top of the bear's head, as well as a collar at the bottom of the head.

Puppy Dog Cake

1 quantity Yogurt Sponge Cake
(see page 16)

1 quantity Buttercream Icing
– white (see page 18)

½ quantity Decorating Marzipan
(see page 22)

pink and green food colouring

icing sugar, for dusting

liquorice string

chocolate dragées

Every child wants a puppy dog. You can help make that dream come true with this charming cake.

Bake the cake mixture in two 23-cm/9-inch round cake tins. Reserve some cake mixture to make 2 standard cupcakes. Leave to cool completely before icing.

Ice the top of one cake. Place the second cake on top and use the remaining icing to ice the cake and the two cupcakes evenly.

Colour two thirds of the decorating marzipan with the pink food colouring, and colour the remainder with the green. Roll out the pink marzipan on a work surface dusted with icing sugar, cut into a long thin strip and wrap this around the large cake to make the dog's collar. Knead together the remainder and form the dog's tongue.

Cut out two small discs of green marzipan for the eyes. Place the tongue and eyes on the cake, as shown on page 33. Use the liquorice string to outline the ears and jowls. Cut one piece of licorice in half and place one half on each eye. Place 3 chocolate dragées on each cupcake paw, and one above the jowls and tongue to form the nose. Scatter the remaining dragées randomly over the cake to create the dog's spots.

Bunny Cake

1 quantity Carrot Cake
(see page 14)

1 quantity Cream Cheese Coconut
Icing (see page 20)

150 g/5½ oz coconut, grated

pink food colouring

jelly discs

jelly fruits

red liquorice string

Not just for birthdays, this cake would be lovely at Easter time as a special treat. Of course, you can colour the coconut flakes any colour you desire.

Bake the cake in a 25 x 30-cm/10 x 12-inch rectangular cake tin. Leave to cool. Using a 13-cm/5-inch round biscuit cutter or glass, cut out 2 circles to form the head and body. Cut out 2 elliptical pieces to form the ears. Cut out 4 equal-sized triangles to form the paws.

Preheat the oven to 150°C/300°F/Gas Mark 2. Ice all the pieces. Place the coconut in a bowl and carefully mix with the pink food colouring. Dry in an oven for 20 minutes. Stir occasionally so that the coconut does not brown. Leave to cool.

Sprinkle the iced cake with the coloured coconut. Arrange the pieces to form the rabbit, either directly on the serving platter or in a gift box. Use the jelly discs and jelly fruits to form the eyes. Use the liquorice string for the whiskers and mouth. Use 2 more jelly fruits for the belly button and nose.

Castle Cake

1 quantity Yogurt Sponge Cake (see page 16)

1 quantity Buttercream Icing – white (see page 18)

yellow food colouring

jelly fruits or jelly tots

1 square biscuit

liquorice string

1½ quantities Decorating Marzipan (see page 22)

red food colouring

orange food colouring

green food colouring

Is your kid crazy about knights and all things medieval? Why not make it a birthday to remember with this authentic Castle Cake? It is sure to impress kids and adults alike.

Bake the cake mixture in two 23 x 13-cm/9 x 5-inch loaf tins. Increase the recipe baking time by approximately 10 minutes. Leave to cool before icing. Dye the icing yellow. Trim all the sides of each cake until they are level and the cakes are rectangular. For the main section of the castle, place one cake on a platter or foil-covered cardboard. Cut the remaining cake in half vertically, and stand on the end of each side of the main section. Attach each end cake piece using about 1 tablespoon of yellow icing and a wooden skewer. Ice the entire castle with yellow frosting. Place approximately one quarter of the icing in a piping bag fitted with a small star-shaped nozzle. Pipe the icing decoratively around the outer edges of the cake. Pipe a line of icing around the entire cake where the cakes are joined.

Decorate with jelly fruits or jelly tots, as shown on page 37. Press the biscuit into one side of the castle to form the gate. Attach 3 short pieces of liquorice to the door with a little icing.

Dye two thirds of the decorating marzipan red. Form spires out of the red marzipan and place on the castle roof. Dye a small amount of the marzipan orange and form 2 pennant flags. Attach each flag to one end of a cocktail stick and stick the cocktail sticks in the cake on either side of the gate. Dye the remainder of the marzipan green and form a long cord. Flatten one edge of the cord with a fork and place along the bottom edge of the castle to form the grass.

Dinosaur Cake

1 quantity Soured Cream Madeira Cake (see page 12)

140 g/5 oz plain chocolate pieces

6 tbsp vegetable shortening or butter

3 quantities Decorating Marzipan (see page 22)

pink food colouring (or any shade you desire)

Just the ticket for the dino-crazy kid in your home. Use artificial trees from model suppliers to create an authentic Jurassic age feeling on the table.

Bake the cake in a heart-shaped tin measuring approximately 33 x 30 cm/ 13 x 12 inches. Leave to cool.

Melt the chocolate and vegetable shortening in a double boiler, or put the chocolate pieces in a heatproof bowl and place over a saucepan of simmering water. The chocolate will melt slowly, so leave it alone (no need to stir) and watch it carefully. Stir in the shortening, keeping the glaze warm in the double boiler.

Cut the cake in half, and then sandwich the halves together using some glaze to bond them. Place the cake on a cooling rack with the rounded side up.

Divide the marzipan in half. Set half aside.

Shape one third of the remaining marzipan into a tail and attach it to the lowest end of the cake. Mould one third into a head-like shape and place it on the other end of the cake. Shape the final third into spikes and a cord the length of the top seam of the cake. Lay the cord over the seam and stud with the marzipan spikes.

Pour the remaining glaze over the cake and leave to cool. Carefully transfer the cake to a serving platter, using a large palette knife to support the entire length of the cake.

Dye half of the remaining marzipan. Mould 4 feet, 2 eyes and a snout out of the coloured marzipan. Mould the remainder into claws, eyebrows and eyeballs. Place these on and around the cake, as shown on page 39.

Smiling Fish Cake

1 quantity Yogurt Sponge Cake (see page 16)

1 quantity Cream Cheese Coconut Icing (see page 20)

1 quantity Decorating Marzipan (see page 22)

blue food colouring

This cake will definitely make an impression, perfect if your kid is a fan of all things aquatic!

Bake the cake mixture in two 20-cm/8-inch round cake tins. Leave to cool completely before icing.

When cooled, ice the top of one of the cakes. Place the second cake on top and use the remaining icing to ice the cake evenly. Use a palette knife to create a wavy surface. If you like, you can omit the coconut from the icing.

Make 2 equal-sized balls and 3 little triangular teeth out of uncoloured marzipan. Dye the remaining marzipan with blue food colouring. Make 2 discs, 2 dorsal fins, and a large tail fin by modelling the marzipan into the required shapes. Roll two pieces of marzipan into thin cords of varying lengths to form the lips. Place the marzipan pieces on the iced cake, as shown on page 41.

Sweet Shop Cake

1 quantity Carrot Cake
(see page 14)

1 quantity Cream Cheese Coconut
Icing (see page 20)

red food colouring, as needed

any assorted sweets such as:

    liquorice pieces

    chocolate drops

    mini-marshmallows

    jelly beans

This cake is fun and versatile; there is no limit to what kind of sweets you can add. Select your favourites and get decorating.

Bake the cake in two 20-cm/8-inch round cake tins and leave to cool before icing and decorating.

Add a few drops of red food colouring to the icing until a pale pink colour is achieved. Cover the top of one cake layer with icing, place the second layer on top and ice the top and sides of the cake. Swirl the icing to create a wavy look. Refrigerate the cake until needed.

Shortly before serving, remove the cake from the refrigerator. Scatter sweets over the entire cake, according to taste. Do not place the cake in the refrigerator once the sweets are on the cake because they will draw moisture and their colouring will begin to bleed into the icing.

Lollipop Cake

1 quantity Banana Cake
(see page 10)

1 quantity Whipped Soured
Cream Icing (see page 21)

assortment of lollipops

1 packet jelly fruits or gum drops
in assorted colours

This is the perfect cake to surprise any child. And best of all, it takes only minutes to decorate.

Bake the cake in a 25 x 30-cm/10 x 12-inch rectangular cake tin. Leave to cool completely before icing.

When cooled, ice the cake evenly all around. Use a palette knife to create a very even surface on top. You can chill the cake at this stage if necessary. Do not refrigerate the cake with the sweet decorations in place because they will draw the moisture and soften.

Place the jelly sweets around the edge of the cake. Insert the lollipops into the surface. Serve immediately.

Flower Petal Cake

1 quantity Yogurt Sponge Cake
(see page 16)

1 quantity Buttercream Icing
– white (see page 18)

malted milk balls, or other small
chocolate sweets

1 quantity Dark Chocolate Icing
(see page 19)

jelly fruits in assorted colours

yellow shoelace liquorice or jelly
string

jelly discs

*There is lots of room for variation with this design. Vary the sweets or colour the white
icing for a different effect – it will always taste delicious.*

Bake the cake in a 25-cm/10-inch round cake tin. Leave to cool completely before
icing.

Cut out the middle area of the cake using a 7.5–10-cm/3–4-inch round biscuit cutter,
glass or bowl. Press down hard and remove the centre portion of the cake. Cut the
remaining outer circle of cake into wedges.

Ice the wedges with the Buttercream Icing. Decorate each wedge with a malted milk
ball. Ice the centre of the cake with the Dark Chocolate Icing. Line the outer edge of
the centre cake with jelly fruits. Create the 'middle' of the blossom with a jelly string,
a jelly disc and jelly fruits, as shown on page 47. Place the centre cake on a platter and
arrange the wedges around it, leaving some space between the centre cake and the
wedges.

Daisy Cake

1 quantity Soured Cream Madeira Cake (see page 12)

1 quantity Buttercream Icing – white (see page 18)

yellow and red food colouring

sugar flowers

button sweets

Perfect for any older girl on your birthday list, this cake is pretty without being too cute. The colouring is your choice: it is equally pretty in white, light blue or pink.

Bake the cake mixture in two 23-cm/9-inch round cake tins. Leave to cool completely before icing.

Dye the icing with the yellow food colouring. Add a few drops of red for a slightly more orange shade. When the cakes are sufficiently cooled, ice the top of one of them. Place the second cake on top of the first and use the remaining icing to cover the cake evenly. Use a palette knife to create a slightly wavy surface.

Distribute the sugar flowers on the top and sides of the cake and scatter the button sweets over the surface.

Strawberry Cake

1 quantity Soured Cream Madeira Cake (see page 12)

red food colouring

2 quantities Whipped Soured Cream Icing (see page 21)

1 quantity Decorating Marzipan (see page 22)

green food colouring

A little trick turns a heart-shaped cake into this fruity birthday treat. Just add a little strawberry syrup to the icing for a delicious twist.

Bake the cake in a 30 x 35-cm/12 x 13-inch heart-shaped cake tin. Leave to cool completely before icing.

Add red food colouring to the icing and mix, creating a dark red. Keep mixing in food colouring until you reach a shade of red you like. Cut the cake in half horizontally. Ice the bottom layer and replace the top. Cover the cake with the remaining icing. Using the tines of a fork, prick the surface to create the 'seeds' of the strawberry.

Dye the marzipan two different shades of green and roll out thinly. Using a pizza wheel, cut the marzipan into leaves and arrange them decoratively at the top of the strawberry, thereby transforming the heart shape into a strawberry shape, as shown on page 51.

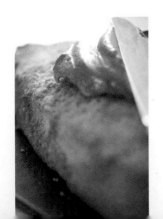

Noughts-and-Crosses Cake

1 quantity Chocolate Cake
(see page 8)

1 quantity Buttercream Icing
– white (see page 18)

red shoelace liquorice

black liquorice pieces

It's every kid's favourite game, and this delicious version will have them asking to play another round!

Bake the cake in a 25 x 30-cm/10 x 12-inch rectangular cake tin. Leave to cool completely, then slice the cake in half horizontally.

Ice the top of one layer, place the other layer on top and ice both together.

Lay 4 lengths of red shoelace liquorice vertically and horizontally across the iced cake to form 9 squares. Use whole shoelace liquorice and liquorice pieces to form noughts and crosses.

Irresistible Chocolate Spider Cake

1 quantity Chocolate Cake
(see page 8)

1 quantity Dark Chocolate Icing
(see page 19)

85 g/3 oz white chocolate chips

1 tsp vegetable shortening

¼ quantity Decorating Marzipan
(see page 22)

cocoa powder, for dusting

red liquorice string

2 small red and white sweets

This deliciously different cake is especially popular with creepy crawly fans and also makes a perfect centrepiece for a Halloween party.

Bake the cake mixture in two 23-cm/9-inch round cake tins. Leave to cool completely before icing.

Ice the top of one cake, place the other cake on top and ice the whole cake. Before the icing hardens, place the white chocolate chips and shortening in a small, zip-top plastic freezer bag. Place in a microwave oven and cook on High for 45 seconds. Squeeze gently and carefully. If necessary, cook for an additional 10–15 seconds; squeeze until the chips have melted. Make a small diagonal cut in a bottom corner of the bag; squeeze the mixture onto the cake to form a series of 4–5 concentric circles.

Using a knife or a cocktail stick, immediately draw 8–10 lines through the circles at regular intervals from the centre to the edges of the cake to form the web.

Shape some marzipan into the spider's body, and dust generously with cocoa powder. Place it in the centre of the web. Use some red liquorice string for legs and small red and white sweets for eyes.

Cook's Tip: if you don't have a microwave oven, melt the chocolate chips in a small bowl over a saucepan of hot water. Place in the plastic bag and proceed with the recipe.

Crazy Banana Cake

1 quantity Banana Cake
(see page 10)

1 quantity Dark Chocolate Icing
(see page 19)

40 g/1½ oz coconut flakes

banana-shaped sweets

popcorn

This cake requires little preparation for the topping, and the unusual addition of the popcorn makes it especially fun to eat.

Bake the cake in a 23-cm/9-inch round cake tin. Leave to cool completely before icing.

Slice the cake in half horizontally. Ice the top of the bottom layer and place the second layer on top. Ice the cake completely.

Sprinkle the sides of the cake with coconut flakes. Decorate the top of the cake with banana-shaped sweets and popcorn.

Football Cake

2 quantities Yogurt Sponge Cake (see page 16)

1 lemon

1 quantity Buttercream Icing (see page 18)

75 g/2¾ oz coconut flakes

green food colouring

175 g/6 oz white chocolate

Score a hat-trick with this great cake. It would be perfect for any aspiring footballer in your family.

Bake the cake in a 33 x 46-cm/13 x 18-inch shallow rectangular cake tin. Leave to cool completely before icing.

Slice the cake in half horizontally. Finely grate the lemon rind and fold into the icing. Coat one layer of the cake with a quarter of the icing. Place the second layer on top and completely ice the cake. Refrigerate.

Preheat the oven to 150°C/300°F/Gas Mark 2. Place the coconut in a bowl and carefully mix with the green food colouring. Dry in the oven for 20 minutes. Stir occasionally so that the coconut does not brown. Sprinkle the coconut over the iced cake.

Chop the white chocolate and melt in a double boiler or in a heatproof bowl set over a saucepan of simmering water. Put into a piping bag fitted with a fine nozzle and carefully pipe the playing field outlines and goal markings onto the cake.

Baseball Cap Cake

1 quantity Yogurt Sponge Cake
(see page 16)

1 quantity Buttercream Icing
– white (see page 18)

green food colouring

1 small orange gum drop or small
jelly fruit

green liquorice string

brown liquorice string

Any sports fan will be delighted to receive this fanciful cap-shaped cake as a birthday treat.

Bake the cake in a 21-cm/8¼-inch ball-shaped cake tin (these are available commercially, or you can use an ovenproof flat-bottomed stainless steel bowl). Leave to cool completely before icing.

Place the cake on a work surface. Using a very sharp long knife, slice a piece about 2.5 cm/1 inch high off the bottom of the cake. Cut this lower section in half (discard the second half or use for another purpose).

Turn the cake flat side down. Align the half-circle of cake along the edge of the round cake on a large tray, trimming to shape the inside of the cake to fit around the sphere, like the peak of the cap.

Colour the icing with the food colouring and ice the cap and peak.

Position a gum drop to represent the button. Use the green liquorice string to make the seams in the cap. Use more green string to shape the number on the peak. Wrap the brown liquorice string along the base of the cake.

Using green liquorice string, write in the team number or the recipient's age.

Play Your Music Cake

1 quantity Yogurt Sponge Cake
(see page 16)

½ quantity Buttercream Icing
– white (see page 18)

cornflour, for dusting

700 g/1 lb 9 oz ready-to-use white
fondant

blue food colouring

Bring yourself right up to date with this delicious personal music player cake, a great idea for older children.

Bake the cake in a 25 x 30-cm/10 x 12-inch rectangular cake tin. Leave to cool completely before icing.

Cut the cake horizontally. Ice the top of one layer, place the second layer on top and thinly ice the remainder of the cake. Dust a work surface with cornflour. Using a rolling pin lightly dusted with cornflour, roll the fondant into a 35 x 40-cm/ 14 x 16-inch rectangle. Carefully lay the fondant over the iced cake and smooth onto the cake. Use a soft brush to dust off any cornflour. Cut the extra fondant overlapping the sides of the cake with a pizza wheel.

Knead half of the remaining fondant again. Shape 2 long cords, and roll the remaining fondant as directed above. Using biscuit cutters or a small knife, cut out into thin strips, 5 triangles and 1 circle.

Dye the remaining fondant light blue. Shape two earphones as shown on page 63. Roll out the remaining fondant and cut into a 10 x 15-cm/4 x 6-inch rectangle and a circle 13 cm/5 inches in diameter. Place on the cake as shown opposite, then decorate with the triangles, strips and circle as shown. Lay the earphone cords on the cake and attach the earplugs. If you have any fondant left over, you can make musical notes, the birthday boy or girl's name, or his or her favourite song title and place this on the blue screen.

Alphabet Block Cake 26

banana cake 10
   Crazy Banana Cake 56
   Lollipop Cake 44
Baseball Cap Cake 60
Bunny Cake 34
buttercream icing 18
buttermilk: banana cake 10

carrot cake 14
   Bunny Cake 34
   Sweet Shop Cake 42
Castle Cake 36
chocolate
   chocolate cake 8
   dark chocolate icing 19
   Dinosaur Cake 38
   Football Cake 58
chocolate cake 8
   Irresistible Chocolate Spider Cake 54
   Noughts-and-Crosses Cake 52
coconut
   Bunny Cake 34
   Crazy Banana Cake 56
   cream cheese coconut icing 20
Crazy Banana Cake 56
cream cheese coconut icing 20

Daisy Cake 48
Dinosaur Cake 38

Flower Petal Cake 46
Flying Balloons Cake 28
fondant: Play Your Music Cake 62
Football Cake 58

icings
   buttercream icing 18
   cream cheese coconut icing 20
   dark chocolate icing 19
   whipped soured cream icing 21
Irresistible Chocolate Spider Cake 54

jelly fruits and gumdrops
   Bunny Cake 34
   Castle Cake 36
   Flower Petal Cake 46
   Lollipop Cake 44
   Sweet Shop Cake 42

liquorice
   Baseball Cap Cake 60
   Bunny Cake 34
   Castle Cake 36
   Flower Petal Cake 46
   Flying Balloons Cake 28
   Irresistible Chocolate Spider Cake 54
   Noughts-and-Crosses Cake 52
   Puppy Dog Cake 32
Lollipop Cake 44

marzipan 22
   Castle Cake 36
   Dinosaur Cake 38
   Flying Balloons Cake 28
   Irresistible Chocolate Spider Cake 54
   Puppy Dog Cake 32
   Smiling Fish Cake 40
   Strawberry Cake 50
   Teddy Bear Cake 30

Noughts-and-Crosses Cake 52

pineapples: carrot cake 14
Play Your Music Cake 62
popcorn: Crazy Banana Cake 56
Puppy Dog Cake 32

Smiling Fish Cake 40
soured cream
   chocolate cake 8
   soured cream Madeira cake 12
   whipped soured cream icing 21
soured cream Madeira cake 12
   Daisy Cake 48
   Dinosaur Cake 38
   Strawberry Cake 50
Strawberry Cake 50
Sweet Shop Cake 42

Teddy Bear Cake 30

walnuts: carrot cake 14

yogurt
   whipped sour cream icing 21
   yogurt sponge cake 16
yogurt sponge cake 16
   Alphabet Block Cake 26
   Baseball Cap Cake 60
   Castle Cake 36
   Flower Petal Cake 46
   Flying Balloons Cake 28
   Football Cake 58
   Play Your Music Cake 62
   Puppy Dog Cake 32
   Smiling Fish Cake 40
   Teddy Bear Cake 30